CITY POEMS

T0159798

CITY POEMS

JOE FIORITO

PREFACE BY A.F. MORITZ

EXILE
editions

Fiction, Poetry, Non-fiction, Translation, Drama and Graphic Books

Library and Archives Canada Cataloguing in Publication

Fiorito, Joe, 1948-, author
City poems / Joe Fiorito ; preface by A.F. Moritz.

Issued in print and electronic formats.
ISBN 978-1-55096-770-8 (softcover).--ISBN 978-1-55096-771-5 (EPUB).--
ISBN 978-1-55096-772-2 (Kindle).--ISBN 978-1-55096-773-9 (PDF)

I. Moritz, A. F., writer of preface. II. Title.

PS8651.I59C58 2018   C811'.6   C2018-900939-X
C2018-900940-3

Second Printing.
Copyright © Joe Fiorito, 2018
Preface copyright © A.F. Moritz, 2018
Design and composition by Michael Callaghan
Typeset in Bembo and Birka fonts at Moons of Jupiter Studios
Cover photo © Joe Fiorito, 2018

Published by Exile Editions Ltd ~ www.ExileEditions.com
144483 Southgate Road 14 – GD, Holstein, Ontario, N0G 2A0

We gratefully acknowledge the Canada Council for the Arts, the
Government of Canada, the Ontario Arts Council,
and the Ontario Media Development Corporation
for their support toward our publishing activities.

 Conseil des Arts du Canada   Canada Council for the Arts

 ONTARIO ARTS COUNCIL CONSEIL DES ARTS DE L'ONTARIO   Ontario   Ontario Media Development Corporation

Canadian sales representation:
The Canadian Manda Group, 664 Annette Street,
Toronto ON M6S 2C8 www.mandagroup.com 416 516 0911

North American and international distribution, and U.S. sales:
Independent Publishers Group, 814 North Franklin Street,
Chicago IL 60610 www.ipgbook.com toll free: 1 800 888 4741

because not even the landlady
could remember their names.

—"The Fire in the Tenement"
Raymond Souster, 1921-2015

Contents

Preface | xiii

(Untitled) | 1

Silent Night on Clarence Square | 2

Moby-Dick | 3

Kevington | 4

Him, and Crack | 5

His Friend Died in the Fire | 6

Her Cracked Lips | 7

sk8rgrl | 8

An Old Queen Recalls (1) | 9

I Go Out on a Party | 10

The Day He Flew | 11

Adam, Eve | 12

I Get It Now | 13

Albino's House | 14

An Old Queen Recalls (2) | 15

He Also Smelled of Lysol | 16

Birthday Present | 17

Buda at the Elgin | 18

Church St. Vernissage | 19

Daphne Bakes a Cake | 20

Brickworks: Dead Dog Day | 21

A Worker's Lament | 22

Dunn Ave. (1) | 23

Dunn Ave. (2) | 24

Ed's Tree | 25

Judy and the Fortune Teller | 26

FTP | 27

He Could Be a Winner | 28

The Hoarder | 29

Him, at the Dentist | 30

Dunn's Ode to Joy | 31

How the Fire Started | 32

Jahman and the Street Nurse | 33

Jami Mosque 9/11 +4 (1) | 34

Jami Mosque 9/11+4 (2) | 35

Karaoke Memorial | 36

Lingerie Football | 37

My Anita | 38

My Pal Al | 39

On the Couch in Pelham Park | 40

On the Sidewalk | 41

Orlando Furioso | 42

Packed Subway | 43

Panhandler's Lament | 44

The Panhandlers' Dispute | 45

Park Bench, Rosedale, Spring | 46

Parkdale Morning | 47

The Parking Lot War | 48

Pho Tau Bay | 49

Pigeon Park, Early Afternoon | 50

Pigeon Park Redux: Life Sucks | 51

RIP Dr. Dru (1) Where He Fell | 52

RIP Dr. Dru (2) The Thai Cook | 53

Roses | 54

Sam Warner Closes Shop | 55

Seaton House, Because | 56

She Killed Him Once | 57

She Walks the Hallway Singing | 58

Spirit Candles Explained | 59

The Carnie in Winter | 60

The Death of Dirty George | 61

The Duchess Works at Night | 62

Her Funeral | 63

The Things You Remember | 64

TSO on Strike | 65

Last Thoughts, Dirty George | 66

Theft Under | 67

Two Girls, Streetcar | 68

Val Ville | 69

Anita, Metro West | 70

Ashlee At Jilly's | 71

An Orange Vest | 72

Sign Language Haircut | 73

Anita in the Alley | 74

Cabbagetown | 75

Everybody Knew | 76

The Robbery | 77

On the Banks of the Credit | 78

The Plain Song of Sammy Yatim | 79

The Old 'Hood | 80

Unpaid Bill | 81

Instructions for the Blackout | 82

Afterword | 85

Notes on the Poems | 89

PREFACE

Joe Fiorito's powerful *City Poems* is new with the freshness of sudden light on what was always beside us, but we became dulled to it, or turned away: it was too constantly troubling, too difficult. Searing in subject matter, profound in meaning and sympathy, the poems are also wonderfully inventive and skillful in poetic form, while remaining casual, colloquial: the art of the street's voice. They're very short: shooting stars. But they constitute pinpoint windows on vast regions, unknown or ignored worlds: struggling people, obscurely dying people, their full reality: the body-and-soul details of pain and loss, endurance, heroism, joys, ugliness and beauty, in the rough corners, wastelands, and crevices where insulted, injured life manages to persist amid the expanse of glass, steel, and money.

The ancient ideal, *maximum in minimo*, much in little, burns in these poems. The book opens with this one, untitled:

> girl in a stairwell:
> burnt spoon, spike,
> lip-froth.
>
> party down the hall
> that's all.

A Japanese *hokku* and *waki* stanza pair, which this resembles, would have been, with its twenty-eight syllables, much too big a suit for Fiorito's spare perception and response. The scene, intensified by the severe condensation, *hits* the reader. Each of the *City Poems* is like this. Yet Fiorito is the very opposite of the poet who depends cheaply on brutal facts for power. The facts are joined with feeling and insight in his abrupt, nervous, almost flayed rhythms, and his expressive sound patterning. On top of this, there's the knife-like tone, ruthless in cutting away all sentiment so that only emotion and vision remain. The progress of the poem points two ways: toward the end, the devastating multiple meanings of "that's all," and back to the beginning, the girl, with the silent sense that she is still—*she especially* is—"the human form divine" (Blake).

"In the naked & outcast Seek Love There," Blake says. In *City Poems*, the outcast come to us and talk. They blink into visibility like a scene suddenly appearing on a black screen of oblivion, their "marginalization," made from our not-knowing. Along with the person at each poem's centre, Fiorito also always provides in a few strokes the person's whole world: friends and tormentors, alleyways or low-rent rooms or parks to sleep in, disasters and sometimes joys.

Anita, Metro West

Me and her in the fountain
when they called the cops on us.
I had a failure to appear.

I'm alone, a little luxury –
two cots per cell; the girls don't
stick together here;

it's ignorant. (No, it's hell.)
She, less guilty minus makeup,
and her freckles in relief…

We hear these people in Fiorito's poems even more powerfully than we see them. We overhear them talking with the marvellous reporter that is Fiorito's poetic presence and voice. We almost become that reporter. "Now I will do nothing but listen," Whitman says, and a little later, "I am the man, I suffered, I was there." Fiorito listens and participates just as surely as does Whitman. If he leaves out all reference to the "I" and any mystical identification with the sufferer, his poetic voice is just as surely and movingly present in each scene, each conversation. The compassion is clear. Co-passio, to suffer with, to experience with.

It's often noted that certain literary writers gained concision, directness, and realistic knowledge from a life in journalism. There are even poets who have made the same comment on themselves. Everyone in Canada ought to know Joe Fiorito as one of our greatest reporters. His *metier* is what the trade dully calls "human interest," and of this he has been a genius. Above all, he has been a communicator: a go-between. The great reporter that Fiorito made himself into, widely observing and profoundly feeling our whole urban society, is the reporter that stands for us in these poems and brings us what he's met.

"Anita, Metro West" shows the approach. Anita speaks for herself; the words are likely edited, paraphrased, but only to pare them to the essence of the voice. Listening, we find ourselves with the reporter-poet in a place where probably we don't go by ourselves: where we doubt that we *can* go. The poet keeps in the background. We might be tempted to call this poetic reporter "humble" but that's not accurate. Simply, he is more interested in Anita than in himself. He might say, if we could interview him, that he exists to meet her and bring news of her. "I had a failure to appear." Isn't that the story of her life, which Fiorito tells by letting her finally tell us?

He doesn't try to erase himself from his encounters. Like ours, his responses are there. It's he who can see her loveliness and pluck. It's he who comments sourly yet tenderly that she is "less guilty minus makeup," a phrase marvellously positioned to mean at least three things: that her "guilt" (her profession of street prostitute) is only a makeup, that her beauty remains and is innocence, and that these two feelings of his are likely also sad awarenesses of her own. When she says that the girls' behaviour in the jail is "ignorant," the aside that "No, it's hell" might just as well be the poet quoting Anita's second thoughts or voicing his own silent response. In fact, it's both. In these poems we feel that the reporter almost becomes the one he meets, while yet he remains separate, the witness, who tells what he sees and so becomes its prophet.

The poems make us see, but we can never forget that Fiorito's main way of witnessing is listening. The word is primary. What can be seen is its context, world: necessary, but not the flower, not the fruit. The people live, they survive (Beckett: "I can't go on, I'll go on") or die, and sometimes in what they say they almost triumph, completing their fates.

Maybe this unique role and power of language is the key to the strange fact of the beauty of these poems. One wouldn't expect poetic beauty from their pitiless subject matter nor from their purposefully brusque, clipped manner, which can often seem sketch-like, almost tossed off or muttered, despite the intense structuring and deep implications that any careful glance reveals. Then, too, there's the tumultuous, creative diction, containing a wealth of knowledge of slang, street culture, the life of drugs, of sleeping rough, of flophouses and tents in ravines, and two dozen other urban categories: not what's usually meant by beauty in literature. But the people speak their own speech in the poems and the human voice is beautiful, especially when it tries its best to say its own unsayable reality, its true self and its total experience.

The people of *City Poems* are always attempting this impossibility. And so are the poems in which the poet must fall back on his own words, as real as theirs, because he has to bring us something so damaged that it has lost its voice and only the poem can provide the "voice" of the now destroyed body and mind:

He Also Smelled of Lysol

this is his bliss:
eating dill fronds
through the fruit stand's

chain-link fence, his lips
like a horse's nibble,
bare feet in a puddle
of his yellow piss.

We could call this cruel, grotesque. What it is is
true. It grasps a whole life in the moment that it has
now come down to. Bliss, ruin and delusion. Ab-
solute reportorial honesty and concision are cou-
pled with a strange brief lyricism, of which sound
patterning is only the most obvious component:
"nibble / puddle / yellow"; and "fronds / stand's";
and "fronds / fruit / fence / feet"; and the way that
the beginning and end, "bliss" to "piss," are linked
via: "dill / his / lips / nibble." "Profound poetry of the
poor and of the dead," says Wallace Stevens. There is
also Fiorito's profound poetry of the poor living dead,
those on the threshold, like this breather of atomized
cleaning fluid.

The book's first sixteen poems form an intro-
ductory group on drug use and damage, though not
every one of them contains this theme. Much of the
last quarter of the book might be thought of as a sec-
tion on "men and women," their catastrophic or
tragic or poignant relationships lived out in Toronto
poverty and homelessness, and the different experi-
ences of the two sexes, their characteristic types of

suffering. But this theme also appears elsewhere. At more than one point in mid-book we encounter pairs of poems that form a man-and-woman diptych: "My Anita" and "My Pal Al," "He Could Be A Winner" and "The Hoarder," for instance. Throughout, there's a constantly astonishing, appalling variety of suffering and human resistance, with many overlappings, interlockings, meaningful juxtapositions and *ritornellos*.

The principal form of the book, then, is to grow more or less like a city grows, and to be drawn together more or less the way an all-curious, passionately concerned traveller draws a thread that eventually links almost everything. It doesn't really matter in what order we read. Wherever we go, we meet a man with a broken back from a catastrophic accident, a poet who lived through the siege of Sarajevo describing how to make candles out of whatever you may still possess, a woman "dry drowning" in her room filled with carefully collected trash, a man turned onto the street from the miserable room where yet he'd been happy, an aging transvestite thinking back, a diseased worker laid off, the thoughts of a thief whose robbery went bad and turned into murder, a prostitute whose alley trick turned into strangulation until she was saved by a stranger who then hit on her, a young drug-user proclaiming her identity "sk8rgrl"...every variety of hopeful hopelessness, of neglect and scorn survived, of homelessness and eviction.

The poems build up an array that becomes the city. When I first began to read the book, I thought perhaps the title wasn't good. Too general: "city poems" could be and are many sorts of things. Quickly I came to feel the title was just right, just as aptly discovered as any of Fiorito's phrasings. Though it seems quiet, really it makes a radical, uncompromising claim: these are the true poems of the city, because what is met in them is city as it is, the real and only city.

As a poet, Fiorito belongs with the modernist questers after the authentic idiom of his place and time. And as with many moderns, his colloquial idiom involves literary depth: we meet Ariosto, we sense Dante almost everywhere, there is *Moby-Dick*, there are allusions to *Genesis* and the *Gospels*, etc., all deployed seamlessly. If the basic technique is a tense free verse, at times it is cut across by riffs of something else: in "Dunn Ave. (2)," the last stanza gives us a moment of the blues; "An Old Queen Recalls (1)" handles the ancient ballad or hymn stanza; "FTP" inventively uses rhymed couplets. But the main poetic tradition is that of William Carlos Williams, including in part the way it was adapted here by Al Purdy. For poetic parallels, alongside *Paterson* I'd point to that great work, *The Spoon River Anthology* by Edgar Lee Masters, and to a poem with the weight and depth of an entire book, Octavio Paz's *I Speak of the City*. Like Williams, Masters, and Paz, Fiorito gathers the seemingly far-flung elements of a community, mainly invisible to each other, into a seething, paradoxically still composition.

Fiorito's book is perhaps the most explicit of these works in insisting that the real humanity is outcast humanity: the despised, the forgotten, the injured and abused, the impoverished. Is *City Poems* great poetry? I don't want to compare greatnesses. The reader will decide. But *City Poems* does focus with a remorselessness all its own on the "man of sorrows and acquainted with grief," the scapegoat. "In the naked & outcast Seek Love There," or in other words,

> In a stairwell, blue-eyed, rough,
> he said he was – until he was
> not – well enough.

—A.F. Moritz
January, 2018

CITY POEMS

girl in a stairwell:
burnt spoon, spike,
lip-froth.

party down the hall
that's all.

Silent Night on Clarence Square

She sewed couture.
He pushed a cart.
She kept a garden.
He slept on the street.

She was soignée.
He smoked a cigar.
They ate Xmas pudding.
She bathed his feet.

Moby-Dick

All the kids have street names:
he is Ahab, Yankee whaler
armed with a harpoon,

marooned on a city street.
"Just trying to get unhooked."
His whale, china white.

Kevington

The boy, in a circle of boys in the yellow light
of a chicken joint at night: "I want rock,
what you got?" – was the thinking there.

A cop to his father: "Come quick,
we think he fell. His head smacked the curb,
our little panhandler."

A medic to his mother: "Be prepared, blood
everywhere." In her panic: "Was he pushed?"
The eventual coroner: "Yes. Or no."

Kevington: no sweeter sweetie, although
he needed to be told to eat, to sleep, to bathe;
told to take his drugs.

Him, and Crack

My wife left when
I came back – Trinidad, my brother,
AIDS-related, dead.

I'm surprised I survived – nice me
then, cruising down River and
Queen, picking them up.

They were all, "Mind if I do this?"
Me, safe: a middle-aged man with
money. By the second week

I had a problem, night and day.
She took my boy. But I had moments –
I can't lie – of joy.

His Friend Died in the Fire

Outside, off and on, for 30 years:
"I'll get" – he said, his front-page grin –
"my in and out." A lock and key.

His friends: "He'll have a bath,
he loves his bubbles." He does so love.
"I had a place once; why live

where they're stabbing you?"
How he got here: "I was sleeping
in a bin; jumped out

just before the dump truck. I'm not
a bad person." His tent was nice,
prior to the fire.

Her Cracked Lips

I lost my daughter
to childhood death; she'd be 32.

It's easier now, numb.
A hit is 10 minutes if it's good.

I'd normally say 10,10, 10 is
the poor man's high.

At the end of the night,
200 bucks. Hurtful? It always is.

I once went 30 days
non-stop.

sk8rgrl

she leans over the sink,
sticks a needle in her neck:
a quick prick,

a slow plunge – eyes
rolled back, her joy lies
in the mirror.

An Old Queen Recalls (1)

My father was a blacksmith,
My mother was a nurse.
I wore her dresses out of doors.
We heard him curse.

My adult life was underground –
a business suit, a vest.
Hallowe'en was a holy day –
lipstick, heels, the rest.

I knew how to make a man
feel good when I took his hand.
"You could, so you did?"
Darling, I still can.

I Go Out on a Party

When she passed out
we dumped her in the stairwell,
dying, dead —

I didn't spike her, didn't
do her — didn't not do her —
so, no assault;

crack whore, little skinny
blondie; spittle, spasm,
not my fault.

The Day He Flew

the snake is his arm
the dog is his leg
the bird is his hair

I spat when he jumped
she sat when he flew
he landed there

Adam, Eve

Do this in memory of him
is the name of the sin.
What was done was not original.

He put it in. You know what
I mean by it, and what
I mean by in.

I Get It Now

She, sucking smoke thru
a glass pipe, gasps.
"You do grass?"

(Who among us hasn't?)
"Ten degrees lower,
three times as fast.'

Albino's House

"I fell and broke my neck" His vertebrae, nubs
in X-rays. He sliced pool cues, fixed them to
his mailbox for something to do – a sign,

like his spine – then onto walls, lintels, fascia –
a transverse process with plastic snakes, spiders,
glued sheep, screwed angels;

look hard for his heroic GI Joe's heroic jeep.
"Do I sleep? At night, in my halo,
a dream before the fall."

An Old Queen Recalls (2)

Michelle Du Barry, feeling blue:
"Cobbler, cobbler, mend my shoe."
Fraught, in New Liskeard

or the Soo. She is a size 9 pump,
an 8 ½ mule. A girl is a woman,
a man is a fool.

Anita Modé – styled like O'Day –
drove the tour bus. Frills and feathers
won't make a nickel miner gay

but: "After the show, a lot of them
wanted me to keep my face on."
She slaps her cheek

rouge-red, recalling a caress.
On a hanger in her closet, sparkle-
pink, pet Juliette's dress.

He Also Smelled of Lysol

this is his bliss:
eating dill fronds
through the fruit stand's
chain-link fence, his lips
like a horse's nibble,
bare feet in a puddle
of his yellow piss.

Birthday Present

Ivor Clive took his sister
for a new bike ride: Hilda Avenue,

13th birthday, summer, after
cake. He led. She lagged. He heard

her back snap when a hot car from
the alley sped. He, broken, spat —

"phht!" – into his fist: "Jesus is
my supervisor – phht!"

and "Where your heart is, there's
your greatest treasure"

Buda at the Elgin

He never said to no one
hello: pockets filled with brushes.
He died alone, melted and

dried: a watercolour of himself.
Here is what he saw: a line of men
under a marquee

in the rain, with the daily late-
edition news, reading
the reviews.

Church St. Vernissage

She was Miss Bar 501,
Miss HOLA, and The Empress
of the Imperial Court.

(Mme. du Barry: "I was Six,
she was Fourteen.")
Tonight, Maria del Monte

in her fruited headpiece – hips,
lips, nips; hard black heels;
green sheath – offers

me the cookie platter. "Would
you like" – her glossy pout –
"chocolate chip?"

Daphne Bakes a Cake

She (a child, then) iced a black cake
with white lime. It set hard, like
plaster; her laughter.

Now come spoons of ginger, sugar,
browning, allspice; Shamrock
wine, one cup.

She broke away to pay the bills,
let me babysit her baby cake,
let me wait, wash up.

"Boy, don't turn your back
upon the door; ambush lurks
or (giggle) evil comes."

Brickworks: Dead Dog Day

Rex ever went to fetch
a ball in the bushes;
this time he backed away.

Then I looked: a dog's head
severed in the purple vetch,
a single dry leaf, blood–

glued to its milky eye,
ears still pricked, black
ants on its tongue.

A Worker's Lament

They didn't treat me bad, not
at first – "We feel for you." – but they
didn't want to watch me itch,

shake out my clothes: "Stay away,
take the other truck, etc." I lost my
ride, I can't afford to move.

His arms, his ankles: star spots,
red dots, black specks on his
cotton sheets.

Dunn Ave. (1)

I didn't mean to hit her.
I mean I guess I did. I mean
I didn't, or else

it was the way she fell.
I didn't keep her in our bed —
I need to sleep —

nor on the couch — my tea,
my *Jeopardy*. I put her in
the bath, because

she leaked and the tub
drains. I washed my hands
in the kitchen sink.

All those people in old movies,
the sound up, late at night?
They are also dead.

Dunn Ave. (2)

In the closet, under her shoes,
the tool kit: coping saw, tin snips,
wire cutters, knife.

I had a trade, a love, a life.
I had to think: how to cut – naked,
or clothed? – my wife.

Naked, then; the trick is not
to think. I mean I thought
I ought to drink.

I bought heavy bags, cut her
in pieces to carry over – where I first
carried her – the threshold.

Arms in the lane, legs behind
the video store, bobbed head in a bin
beside the roti shop; drop.

Cried last night, the night before;
trucks come tomorrow,
try not to cry no more.

Ed's Tree

The catalpa, its leaves big as plates.
"You could not knock it over."
Nor ice, nor age, nor rage

but ants, a ragged line from a labial
scar. A rigging rope holds 5,000 lbs.
Birds and squirrels, un–

nested, confused; also bees and
the raccoon's hole. Seedpods –
unlike the chainsaw's

gasoline – smell green;
how much light this lets in
we'll see.

Judy and the Fortune Teller

Odella, motherly; me, vulnerable.
I saw her for two years, once a week:
"Call before you come."

Crystals, candles, and incense when
she made me write my name
backwards: yduJ.

I liked her mouth, the way she said
I'd dream of him; when I did,
she grew excited then.

FTP

I had a hammer and was laid to rest
with cop bullets in my chest.

I had a knife and waggled my cock;
was shot dead with a service Glock.

I waved scissors in a thin blue hospital
gown; cops took me down.

They said I had a gun; it was a phone.
I clutched my guts and died alone.

Cops sat on me. I was goaded.
Twisted my neck; my chest exploded.

I waved my pellet gun and asked for
the phone-a-friend; bang-bang, the end.

So many stories. So fucking sad.
I am not crazy. I am mad.

He Could Be a Winner

The old man had anger:
I said, "Don't send money." He said,
"Do your job."

I did my job,
sending the money to claim
his prize; his wife so sick,

and him a million-dollar winner
waiting here all day.
We closed at six.

The Hoarder

Her foot, a fist or lotus,
fish-pale, knuckled, bare;
her, breast-stroking

from couch to bath amid
toys for the unborn,
old papers, family pics,

past-due bills, plastic singing
Xmas cards: we call this
dry drowning.

To whit, her legs tucked up:
"In my heart I know
I'm sunk."

Him, at the Dentist

Tenzin Gyatso had a tooth
pulled in Toronto; dope, you hope
it was the wisdom.

Japa malas – the prayer beads of Tibet –
are made of coral, gold, rattan seeds
(moon and stars), or

the skulls or bones of monks: ergo
is the 14th Dalai Lama's jaw a sutra:
bliss, and emptiness.

Dunn's Ode to Joy

I'll drink from, he said, your shoe —
his birthday, her Nikes, baby
duck: her dirty look.

I blushed. Did he? I know
schoolgirls, daily who, hoping
to see a suicide —

up your skirt, missy — saw
instead him run laps below
the viaduct,

Ode to Joy on his shoulder.
He kept a photo of his mother,
turtledove in hand,

PEACE on a faux-satin sash,
her New Year's end-of-war tiara.
We oohed, awed,

sang songs to him and her
with cake crumbs underfoot,
his cup undrunk.

How the Fire Started

"I was thinking fifty times,
the candle – I was thinking fifty times,
my cat, fat like pitulica."

It was not. "This is my coat.
I gave to my son. He gave to his wife.
She gave to me after the fire."

Her cigarettes and chamomile
again, and *Stars* in new heaps
on her balcony.

Jahman and the Street Nurse

With his hands, all his life, hard,
Jahman said he worked; now the nurse
(his weak leg, black lung,

swollen finger) worked on him.
(Did she come from the south with
her big yabba mouth?)

He rapped and shook his natty
beaded dreads. "Weak battery."
Pacemaker? "Nah, man."

His red-red scooter, dead: a boost
from her for it and him, dipped in
the healing stream.

Jami Mosque 9/11 +4 (1)

Arms bare, barefoot, smoking
on her porch: "Those people are — "
in so many words — "us."

Camera, mic boom, cables, cabbies,
bike cops staking out the mosque
across the street.

She said, "They leave their doors
wide open. My cat — " pink tongue
licking ankle salt —

"wanders in; they know her well."
She, tanned, once went where
the women hide their hair.

"The men are nice, never gripe,
instead they bring her here —
put that in the news."

Jami Mosque 9/11+4 (2)

"I was in Libya, teaching,
when the Americans
bombed."

First thought, best
thought? "Were any of my
students killed?

"The people were lovely,
offered help, even though – "
None dead; let it go.

A silver 747 flying overhead;
I saw the contrail, heard
the call to prayer.

Karaoke Memorial

His was the Voice of Thunder –
"You Got Another Thing Coming,"
and "Silent Lucidity" –

until the night he slid off his chair –
big belly, bald spot, barrel chest,
salt&pepper beard,

aneurysm. "His Cocker was
the real Joe." He'd do anything for
a friend, even if it meant

talking wrestling story lines
into the early a.m. "Our best thing,
'Soul Man' – my Sam, his Dave,

never once did he break kayfabe –
though for a while he thought
I stole the show."

Lingerie Football

—R.I.P., R.B. F.

she's quick off the ball,
blonde, tan, hard, tall; me, if I'd been
a girl.

bra and panties, ribbons; bra and
panties, ribbons; three-
point stance

in lipstick, eye-black, pigtails —
my brother's daughter — what is
wrong with me?

My Anita

Plate-glass table, freckled cheek,
bad date – smash, crash, face
slashed. I bet her baby boy

howled; you bet I didn't ask.
She said she gave him up, or
else they took him.

In thrift-store cut-offs, pixie
hair, torn tee – a quickie with
a box-cutter bagged

beneath the tissues in her purse –
she gulped my cold jugged milk.
Her scar zig-zagged.

My Pal Al

To the market once a week
for a week of frozen mini-meals,
a coffee and the paper.

In a puddle of daylight
on white arborite he tore his *Star*
into long thin strips:

"Nobody reads the news
on my dime." He was the news
when he came home:

new lock, no key; no microwave,
no plastic fork and spoon, no
coffee pot, no cot.

In a stairwell, blue-eyed, rough,
he said he was – until he was
not – well enough.

On the Couch in Pelham Park

She had many kids
by many men – seven, and four –
to see her is to know why.

Her boy, bound to get shot –
it's the odds at night, alone here,
coming home: *pop, pop,*

drop the Xbox, run for it.
His wound, still open; her bare
legs, tucked up under.

On the Sidewalk

"How hard is it?" Bosnia, bodies,
bullets, booze; the Princess Pats,
demobbed in Quebec –

no address, so no pension.
"Bosnia?" He raised his shirt;
a scar, you can't fake that.

Orlando Furioso

Here we go again: boy Orlando
hooked by his heels in the garbage
chute, his echo

22 storeys deep – chicken
smells, carrot scraps, eggshells –
"Help me,

I'm going to fall." Bradamente has
AIDS, the Este family sells crack,
Ruggiero keeps pigeons –

so, no help. This I hear now: furioso,
at night, when I have dreams
of falling.

Packed Subway

"I know you're coming to my home
tonight to rape me."
He read his paper.

"You're a pedophile and a rapist."
Next stop, turning page;
giggling, her girl gang.

"I don't know why you say that.
I don't do those things."
He also blushed.

A straphanger: "You don't know
him." The girl said:
"Bitch."

Panhandler's Lament

I'm in the book. I have a room.
The wound is healed. (I assaulted a door

looking for my cat.) The charges
were withdrawn. My cat's name is Bella.

I have a single hotplate, not allowed.
I have one anyway because

you've got to eat. I make 20 bucks
a day; still my fridge is empty.

Put me in jail? I had a tent in Tent City.
That was jail enough.

The Panhandlers' Dispute

His lobster hand:
"I spilled a pot of boiling oil."
His shin red, also.

Sotto voce, blocks along:
"He's lying: someone
poured a pot on him."

The way he held his cap,
the way his fingernails
had melted.

Park Bench, Rosedale, Spring

Wind in the hair of the boy
at play near the ravine. (Go Anywhere
On Greyhound. Sex For Life.)

"They used to call me Annie, and
I hated it. My mother said, when we
came here, 'It isn't England.'"

It is not. "We had a cook –
egg on toast, a bowl of soup – gave me
crusts for geese."

Snowsuit people; last year's leaves.
"A little arthritis." Where's your coat?
"This is my coat, but

I lost my cane; three or four days, said
the Lost&Found. It's now been four.
It must be stolen."

Parkdale Morning

I, too, sleep like that: on my side,
knees bent, head resting
on one arm.

Who bore him named him
Sultan – strength or power,
pearl of rulers –

and would have had him sleep
on silk, not in this park
on a bed of grass,

no wreath of aromatic herbs
but cop tape for his ribbons,
red dew in his curls.

The Parking Lot War

"I don't know the rules."
Gashaw, his wrist cast in plaster:
his wife zipped his zipper.

A night game: "My lot is near
Ryan's — when I flash my light, cars
come to me.

"Ryan said 'Nigger,' named me shit,
shit, hit and hit me, he said,
'Go back there.' I never knew

my hand was not working.
If I go back there, where
do I go?"

Pho Tau Bay

red nails red toes green
dress black hair red lips:
"You like my pho?"

(Yes, and your high collar
too.) "Everything okay,
Joe?" On the Friday:

had she seen *Titanic*?
Her hiss: "I seen a lot
of people drown,

slip under water —
why see again? You go now,
come another time."

Pigeon Park, Early Afternoon

She, sleepy, washed herself there
in a fountain on the square.
I saw what some men

pay to see: skirt up,
leg up, knee raised on the basin.
She pressed a button,

water gushed; she dried herself,
I think, a little roughly. A thirsty
man, a minute later –

his lips at the stream.

Pigeon Park Redux: Life Sucks

Single men sitting
in the dark listening
to Guy Clark,

cigarettes and
brown-bagged drinks,
life stinks.

His hat said "I'd rather
be here dead than
home in bed."

RIP Dr. Dru (1) Where He Fell

In a doorway by the Thai joint
(how hard was it to cut him?)
he leaked blood.

The stain, now washed and dried,
is hidden under candles, flowers,
burger boxes

and a ragged written RIP. "He
stuck up for some mouthy bitch."
A bun in her oven,

kids yap – "Slut," etc., and,
"Who the fuck are you?" The Thai
cook: "Too bad. So sad."

RIP Dr. Dru (2) The Thai Cook

"My sister said
don't look. I looked — a lot
of blood —

he took his coat off where
he fell. I was dizzy,
almost fell.

We put teenage food —
pop and chips, chocolate —
at the temple;

we don't put flowers in
my country." The cops
moved kids along.

Roses

They cost me a buck apiece. I sell them
for three: this one with red panties

sells for five; the one with the pin-light
and two AA batteries, also five.

(He tents his blanket, fumbles in his lap.)
I gotta water my horse – humiliating,

but if I move my chair I lose my spot.
I got this (a sawed-off bat) from a guy

in a bar. "For protection?" said the cop.
(His trickle.) "It's my tire-checker."

Cops do not buy roses.

Sam Warner Closes Shop

I'll go down to Florida. Or I got
a place up north. Or take a cruise:
Russia, Poland.

I had a cop once buy five suits.
(A detective, his promotion;
or a rookie.)

This hat – you're 7 ⅜ – is older
than you. That's a stretcher.
(Like the Greek theta.)

It's time: the parking's bad,
the lighting's bad, the guy next door
wants to expand.

Seaton House, Because

on a field trip
in the valley, school kids
and vets on blankets
near each other.

this boy points, agape:
"that's one of the men
who sleeps with
my mother."

She Killed Him Once

I come from a country
in shit up to my knees – don't want

to complain, don't want to be
deported, but I know her.

I'm here as long as she is here,
even longer. Her place, 24/7

is a crack house, is a whore house –
she gets money, her dealer gets

money hundreds of times. I've been –
with guns and dogs – threatened.

Shots fired, what to do? Nothing.
Sleep in the tub.

She Walks the Hallway Singing

she had the kind of thoughts
tin hats won't prevent.
your green nightie

would be stained, front and
back, if you did, too;
and her arms,

her hair, her bitten nails.
hold your breath to halt
the smell and call

for help; no answer. "Press
two for French";
merde.

Spirit Candles Explained

green for greener
pastures: I mean money.
red draws love.

evil has nine spaces for
the nine names
of the nine sufferings.

love me; fast luck;
come to me; keep the devil
from my home;

or the reversing candle:
what you light against me
sets fire on you.

The Carnie in Winter

"I've had five Roller
Bowlers; this one's the best."

Penny a pitch: too slow, you lose;
trop rapide, whoops:

done right: winner, gagnant,
ding, ding, ding.

This is the Tornado: I imagine
you puke. "You do."

With his Texas reader, with his
Svengali act and with

his summer whack-a-mole
he does all the malls.

The Death of Dirty George

He took one on the jaw,
said he feared he'd take one there.

"He fucking pushed me,"
said the super to a neighbour, unafraid.

George fell, called, wept, sprawled
on the couch: his spiders were patient.

The smell got kitchen-scraps bad.
His spiders: "He's not so big now."

The Duchess Works at Night

The Duchess is a tugboat in a slip
or an ant in a jewel box.

Como, I'm touching you –
it's all just rubber. Careful captain:
"Good, thanks."

Rub that off, she's looking good.
We've stirred up bodies –
once, a little girl.

The anchor, dragging,
is a pivot. "*Duchess*, push full."
A rooster tail of water

under the sparkling moon.
"Thank you, Captain."
All lines slack.

Her Funeral

Melody, next to the tracks
sat by a dry twig fire with a tallboy
in a paper sack –

"She died on my day off.
She had a photographic memory –
look you in the eye,

draw your face." Also: "If we had
beers and woke up rough –
her hangover soup, very

whatnot, was the best." And?
"This is her medicine bag: stones,
a bird, a lighter, cigarettes."

– until there came a fast train:
squint and listen to the cinders
say her name.

The Things You Remember

The drugs go up your ass
or in your arm: four-point restraints.
"Excuse me?"

You sweat like a pig and
go into a coma if you don't get
fruit juice. I got the juice

three times a day for sixty days.
My crime? Dropping out of classes
during the missile crisis.

Electrodes, mouth guards and –
nothing. All I remember now
is that I forget.

TSO on Strike

Her hickey, a mark of
the violin. Who has this bow
spent fifteen grand.

No looty, no cosi fan tutti
says the Jukka-Pekka
polka band.

A min-wage arpeggio
as the cellist breastfeeds
in the rain.

Last Thoughts, Dirty George

I thought she'd go before me –
wrong again. In the space
between heartbeats

I am free – two, three – to see
grace in a spider's web;
lamp glint on the kettle's

curve; letter slot, metal door;
bug on floor; tobacco ash.
I am wisps of grey,

inhaling the last of myself
from familiar pores
no more.

Theft Under

A guy hit him, stripped
his wallet, tossed his papers
and took off;

his bloodied face.
She knelt to help, because?
"I knew him from the street."

She gathered his things, called
9-1-1, kept his health card
for the ambulance;

blood drops on her Val Ville top
when he woke up; he's saying,
"Hey, gimme my stuff."

Cop hands spread her legs.
"I got assault, theft under,
failure to appear."

Two Girls, Streetcar

"I'm not, like, hitting
on you" – when we were young
we were joined

at the hip – "my mother still
doesn't trust you" – we were
mean in school.

I am now old – road not
taken; trousers rolled; red
wheel barrow and

petals on a wet, black back-
pack: the apparition of these
girls at Ossington.

Val Ville

I strut a dead man's boots –
no idea who he was,
or where he walked;
there, here?

Do boots remember steps,
miss their master's
double-knotted laces,
fallen arches, work socks?

What is the right word
for sadness, cracked leather,
my warm foot instead
of his?

Anita, Metro West

Me and her in the fountain
when they called the cops on us.
I had a failure to appear.

I'm alone, a little luxury –
two cots per cell; the girls don't
stick together here;

it's ignorant.(No, it's hell.)
She, less guilty minus makeup,
and her freckles in relief:

I'm doing as much cell time
as I can. Grey sweats, plump
cheeks, scars less sharp.

We eat box potatoes –
the males cook it and the females
eat it: her metaphor.

Ashlee at Jilly's

The stripper's hand is also firm.
"Would you like a dance
today?" Not today.

She plays a handheld "Wheel
of Fortune" – due to copyright,
there is no wheel, so it is

naked on-line "hangman"
at the bar; misses Shenandoah Valley,
nails Automatic Teller.

"Your next girl, Ashlee, queen
of hearts." Music up, game
done, wheel down.

An Orange Vest

The three men with a backhoe
under the black branches of

this tree – how can you not be
happy, how can you not want

his orange vest, his blue hard hat,
his jack hammer, as passing men

or as women in high heels in
such a tight space do.

Sign Language Haircut

short back and sides?
he can't ask can't hear
can't see but can

feel the scissors' snip,
the whisk, brush stiff
as stubble.

the barber holds his hand
and tells him he is yet again
a handsome man.

Anita in the Alley

"I said 'sure' to him,
figuring twenty minutes
of touching;

then he was strangling me."
Her thumbs on my
Adam's apple,

by example.) "No one helped."
Until a guy helped; then?
"He hit on me."

Cabbagetown

The strip steaks in the freezer
are hot and cheap the lot; so what,
my teeth are shot.

Mostly I'm here for a beer
at noon – the A/C, TV sports,
the Sunshine girl.

It beats my bachelor –
nom de plume for a single room –
mine's gloom and doom.

It's laughter in the bar.
I splash in the pisser in slippers –
no mopping here.

Everybody Knew

He kept his money in a sock –
hold on, who does the sock anymore?
He did; worse, he said he did;

worst, he thought it clever to say.
Until she came home, arm in arm,
to sit on him.

The sock: he'd read it in a book.
His arms: she pinned them down.
He clawed the air.

About the air: unclawable.
She left him there and bought
a week of drinks, etc.

for friends. First the swelling,
then the smell , then 911.
His missing sock?

Proof absence is proof of nothing
said the cops, who learned
she cleared her tab.

The Robbery

1. I wasn't going to (my knife
at her throat) cut;
she didn't know that.

2. He said open the safe.
Her neck, soft; his blade,
a rape icicle.

3. She opened the safe.
Not much money,
just some.

On the Banks of the Credit

where the salmon spawn
by the river's edge

the leaves are sloppy rotten
after the snow melt:

red birds there, alder and
wolf track, wisps

of yellow tape where,
in the twitch grass, lay

the body of the girl.

The Plain Song of Sammy Yatim

My knife, music in the air:
the sound, in slo-mo, as the buzz of bees,
the ripping of a seam

or a silver zipper, mine, indecent
in descent; so what? I'd say I was tired but
you're asking the wrong guy.

"Pussy!" was the downbeat to Forcillo's
Glock descant – *tack, tack, tack* – a prelude
to six more hot ones

and in the silence of the sirens came
Pravica, counting the diminuendo
with his taser.

The Old 'Hood

The hedgehog died, the translator
cried, the lady across the street
leaned, with radio frequency,
on her horn.

A cardinal rule is to make a lot of
noise; tweet tweet means I am
sweet on a date.

Do you hear the siren?
A man down the block grows onions
on his lawn. Last year it was corn,

he lost his view of the other side
of the street. Once I saw him
weeding, sarong hiked.

Unpaid Bill

He snaked a discarded string
of Xmas lights – red, green, red,

blue – from a plug-in down the
hall, slithered under

his door after the landlord cut
light and heat. He made coffee

with that cord, read his papers;
blinking didn't bother him.

Instructions for the Blackout

Keep old wax and make
another candle; the best wick
is a shoelace.

Or, if you have olive oil –
half a glass – use a wine cork
float, threaded with

cord. For some reason
the phone lines are always live:
to hook up a transistor,

strip the wires, connect
negative to negative and get
a flicker of the news.

AFTERWORD

The intersection of Sherbourne and Dundas Streets in Toronto is known as Cash Corner. It is where contractors come to pick up day labourers from among the hard and skinny homeless men.

If you are chosen you hop into a truck and head off to tear apart a kitchen, to rip asbestos from a ceiling, or to haul old boilers out of factories which are being converted into lofts. You get dropped off on the corner, cash in hand, when the day is done.

Don't tell me drunks don't work hard.

One morning I saw a young man walk by the assembled crowd: wife-beater, do-rag, pants hanging off his ass, hard muscles, and tattoos. He was as wary of the homeless men as he was of me; wary of them because of fate; wary of me because I could be a cop.

I didn't stare at him, but as he passed I watched closely. There was a tattoo of a man's face on his shoulder. A rapper? A dead brother? A fallen friend? The face looked familiar. I was puzzled by that familiarity. And then it hit me. The tattoo was of his own face.

That's a poem.

The poems gathered here are images which remain from my time as a newspaper columnist. The debt runs deeper than that experience: I owe Raymond Souster, Toronto's city poet, who remains my example. I owe W.W.E. Ross, whose imagist poems I fell for early. And I owe Barry Callaghan for his gruff encouragement.

Thanks also to Michael Redhill and Stuart Ross for their early advice and counsel; and, if I may reach back to the beginning, thanks to that gang of poets in Montreal.

—Joe Fiorito

NOTES ON THE POEMS

p. 1: Her name was Mew-Mew; this time, she was saved by a shot of naloxone.

p. 3: China white is a powerful mixture of heroin and fentanyl.

p. 4: His parents still don't know if it was murder.

p. 5: In those days, when there was a major marijuana bust in Toronto, the dealers would offer crack as a cheap alternative.

p. 9: The history of gay Toronto in the Fifties, in a nutshell.

p. 10: The death of Mew-Mew

p. 13: An explanation of the attraction of crack cocaine.

p. 16: Lysol, from a spray can, for sniffing. I never saw him again after that summer.

p. 18: Janos Buda died in his apartment; the body was not found for six months. He was a noted artist in Hungary; in Toronto he painted signs for Honest Ed Mirvish. In retirement, Buda made watercolour sketches of the city. His apartment was filled to the ceilings with stacks of his work at the time of his death.

p. 22: When bedbugs came to Toronto.

p. 26: Judy, a normal person, spent $5,000 for the counsel of Mme. Odella, the fortune teller.

p. 31: Fred Dunn lived in a tent in a ravine. He was a fitness fanatic who ran laps around a homemade track, barefoot, all year long, while carrying an 85-lb. log; he called the log his Ode to Joy.

p. 32: Lily's fire occurred one Christmas Eve when a lit cigarette, tossed from a balcony above, landed on her balcony. Pitulica is a Macedonian meat pie. The firemen said the cat did not suffer.

pp. 34, 35: Scenes from a press conference at a mosque in the west end of Toronto, in the aftermath of the Twin Towers.

p. 37: Former Toronto mayor Rob Ford's niece played in the Lingerie Football League. He watched her games.

p. 39: Al Gosling was evicted from public housing because he neglected to fill out some paperwork. He caught an infection in a shelter and died not long after. The woman who began the proceedings against him was promoted.

p. 56: This is one of the creation myths of Seaton House. Most of the men in the ravine in those days were veterans of the Second World War, suffering from what we now know as post-traumatic stress disorder; they couldn't adapt to life on civvy street. The citizens of Toronto built Seaton House to take care of them.

p. 61: Dirty George declined to bathe: if you could stand his smell, you could be his friend. He was beloved by many.

p. 63: I spent an afternoon drinking with Melody and her friends by the railroad tracks near the Summerhill liquor store. She died not along after. My memory of the funeral is wedged between my memory of that afternoon.

p. 65: Jukka-Pekka Saraste was the conductor of the Toronto Symphony Orchestra at the time of the strike. He left Toronto not long after, complaining among other things that he didn't want to raise his child in a city he did not consider sufficiently cultured.

p. 67: Val Ville is Value Village, a used-clothing chain.

p. 73: The man getting the haircut cannot hear, is blind and cannot speak. The barber was gentle.

p. 78: Cecilia Zhang was kidnaped, murdered and dumped. I was curious to see where she was found.

p. 79: In the summer of 2013 Sammy Yatim, a teenager, exposed himself on a Toronto streetcar and flashed his pocketknife at passengers. The streetcar stopped and was safely cleared, but within seconds of the arrival of police, Yatim was shot to death. Constable James Forcillo was later convicted of attempted murder. No charges were laid against Sgt. Dan Pravica for the use of a taser on the body of the mortally wounded boy.

p. 81: The man who snaked the cord is the same man who burned his hand in boiling oil.

p. 82: The advice is from Goran Simic, who survived the siege of Sarajevo.